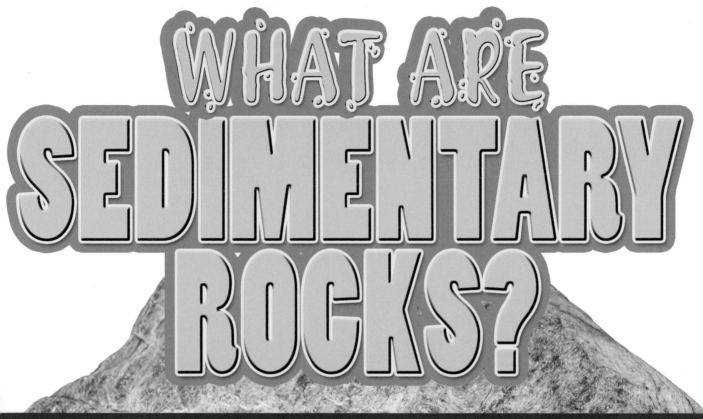

JUNIOR GEOLOGIST
Discovering Rocks, Minerals, and Gems

WHAT ARE SEDIMENTARY ROCKS?

JENNIFER CULP

Britannica
Educational Publishing

IN ASSOCIATION WITH

ROSEN
EDUCATIONAL SERVICES

Published in 2016 by Britannica Educational Publishing (a trademark of Encyclopædia Britannica, Inc.) in association with The Rosen Publishing Group, Inc.
29 East 21st Street, New York, NY 10010

Distributed exclusively by Rosen Publishing.
To see additional Britannica Educational Publishing titles, go to rosenpublishing.com.

First Edition

Britannica Educational Publishing
J.E. Luebering: Director, Core Reference Group
Mary Rose McCudden: Editor, Britannica Student Encyclopedia

Rosen Publishing
Phil Wolny: Editor
Nelson Sá: Art Director
Nicole Russo: Designer
Cindy Reiman: Photography Manager
Phil Wolny: Photo Researcher

Library of Congress Cataloging-in-Publication Data
Culp, Jennifer, 1985– author.
What are sedimentary rocks?/Jennifer Culp.—First edition.
        pages cm.—(Junior geologist : discovering rocks, minerals, and gems)
Includes bibliographical references and index.
ISBN 978-1-68048-241-6 (library bound) – ISBN 978-1-5081-0046-1 (pbk.) – ISBN 978-1-68048-299-7 (6-pack)
1. Sedimentary rocks—Juvenile literature. 2. Geology—Juvenile literature. I. Title.
QE471.C85 2016
552.5—dc23
                                                                                                2015022420

Manufactured in the United States of America

Photo credits: Cover, p. 1 © iStockphoto.com/Rinelle; cover and interior pages background Robert Adrian Hillman/Shutterstock.com; p. 4 James Steinberg/Science Source; p. 5 Print Collector/Hulton Archive/Getty Images; p. 6 Andrew Rakoczy/Science Source; p. 7 Robert and Jean Pollock/Science Source; p. 8 Earth Satellite Corporation/Science Source; p. 9 Dirk Wiersma/Science Source; p. 10 Spencer Sutton/Science Source/Getty Images; p. 11 Portland Press Herald/Getty Images; p. 12 Martin Shields/Science Source; pp. 13, 16 DEA/Archivio J. Lange/De Agostini/Getty Images; p. 14 DEA/C. Bevilacqua/De Agostini/Getty Images; p. 15 Theodore Clutter/Science Source; p. 17 Mint Images – Frans Lanting/Getty Images; p. 18 N. R. Rowan/Science Source; p. 19 David McNew/Getty Images; p. 20 Mark Garlick/Science Source; p. 21 Joe Tucciarone/Science Source; p. 22 George Bernard/Science Source; p. 23 Tommaso Boddi/WireImage/Getty Images; p. 24 © Aurora Photos/Alamy Stock Photo; p. 25 Phil Hill/Science Source; p. 26 Richard and Ellen Thane/Science Source; p. 27 Universal Images Group/Getty Images; p. 28 David R. Frazier/Science Source; p. 29 © Stephen Mulcahey/Alamy Stock Photo; interior pages (arrow) Mushakesa/Shutterstock.com.

CONTENTS

SURFACE ROCK

Earth is made of three different types of rock: igneous, metamorphic, and sedimentary. Earth's crust is made mostly of igneous and metamorphic rocks. Sedimentary rock lies on top of the crust, forming most of Earth's surface.

Sedimentary rocks are formed of tiny particles of minerals, sand, dirt, mud, and even little bits of animal matter, such as bone and the shells of dead sea creatures. These particles are moved by weather

Tiny particles of sediment add up to form mighty rock structures, like this one displaying several different layers deposited over many years.

Shell fossils are visible in this limestone. Limestone makes up about 10 percent of all sedimentary rock.

and water until they settle in one place, combined together. This settled matter is called sediment. Over thousands of years, the particles of sediment are compressed and bonded together to form solid rock. Sedimentary rock forms in layers, and the layers are visible in the existing rock.

Think About It

Sedimentary rock is the most common type of rock you see on the ground outside each day.

HOW ROCKS ARE MADE

Some sedimentary rocks are made when water, wind, and other natural forces cause rocks and earth to wear away. These forces also move bits of rock and earth to new places. In the new place, pressure causes them to bond together. Sometimes dissolved minerals seep into the spaces between the particles. These minerals can harden

The process of erosion leaves a layer of new rock in the bottom of a valley.

into a kind of cement, gluing the particles together into a layer of rock.

As noted earlier, other sedimentary rocks are formed from the bones and shells of animals and sea creatures. After sea creatures die, these bits and pieces fall to the ocean floor, where they become compressed and form rock.

Sedimentary rock is also formed when a body of water *evaporates*, or dries up, leaving the minerals contained within the water behind to harden into rock.

Steam is water in gas form, and it is created when water evaporates from a body of water, such as this river.

WHAT'S THE DIFFERENCE?

As you have learned, sedimentary rock forms from tiny particles of other rock, sand, and organic matter. The other two kinds of rock form in different ways.

Igneous rock is formed from a very hot fluid-like substance called magma. Magma is sometimes described as molten (melted) rock. When magma cools and hardens, it becomes igneous rock. Most of Earth's crust beneath the surface is made up of igneous rock.

Igneous rock, like this landscape shown via satellite, is made up of magma that has cooled and hardened.

Compare and Contrast

How is sedimentary rock different from igneous and metamorphic rock? How is it alike?

Metamorphic rock is formed when sedimentary or igneous rocks are affected by great temperatures and pressures, causing them to change their forms or crystal shapes. Marble is a metamorphic rock formed when the sedimentary rock limestone changes due to high heat and pressure.

Metamorphic slate rock is formed by the high temperatures and pressures in Earth's crust.

THE ROCK CYCLE

Some of the tiny fragments in sediment that eventually become sedimentary rock are themselves made of rock. How is this possible?

Rock is always being formed, worn down into pieces, and then formed again. This process, which takes millions of years, is called the rock cycle. Existing rock wears down through erosion. Fragments of eroded rock then settle down and slowly become sedimentary rock.

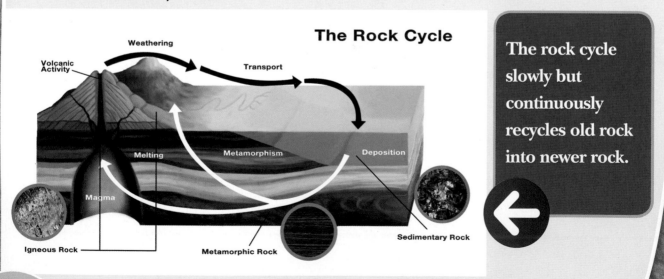

The Rock Cycle

Weathering

Transport

Volcanic Activity

Melting

Metamorphism

Deposition

Magma

Igneous Rock

Metamorphic Rock

Sedimentary Rock

The rock cycle slowly but continuously recycles old rock into newer rock.

If sedimentary rock becomes deeply buried, it can melt into magma, which may return to the surface as igneous rock. Deeply buried sedimentary or igneous rock may also become affected by heat and pressure and change into metamorphic rock.

Think About It

The rock cycle repeats endlessly to form new rock from old rock. How might fragments of an old metamorphic rock eventually become sedimentary rock?

Geologists study rocks and the complex processes that form them.

TYPES OF SEDIMENTARY ROCK

Scientists classify (that is, group together) sedimentary rock into several types, depending on the way they were formed and the kinds of particles that went into them.

One main group is clastic rocks. Clastic means that they are formed from pieces of other rocks, such as gravel, sand, and dirt. There are three general kinds of clastic rock. Conglomerates are formed of larger particles held together by dissolved minerals that act as cement. The individual particles in

Sandstone often has a grainy texture and thus often feels sandy to the touch.

conglomerates can be as large as boulders. Sandstones are made up of small grains of sand that measure between 0.002 and 0.08 inch (0.06 and 2 millimeters). That's smaller than the period at the end of this sentence. Mudstones are very smooth rocks made of even tinier particles than sand.

The fine grains of mud and silt that make up mudstone make it smooth.

Compare and Contrast

How would a conglomerate rock feel different in your hand than sandstone? If you found a very smooth rock that wasn't lumpy, gravelly, or grainy (like sand), what type of rock would you think it is?

Mudstones include shale, which is the most common type of sedimentary rock.

Sedimentary rocks that are formed from organic plant or animal material are known as biochemical. Some limestones are examples of biochemical sedimentary rock; they are formed from the shells of dead sea creatures. Coal is another example.

Remains of creatures found in sedimentary rock are called fossils. Rock can preserve fossils for millions of years.

Quartz is an example of a chemical sedimentary rock made up of inorganic materials.

Chemical sedimentary rocks are formed when inorganic minerals—that is, minerals that do not come from a plant or animal—gather at the bottom of a body of water, where they eventually bind together to become rock. Rock salt is an inorganic sedimentary rock.

Vocabulary

Organic matter comes from living things. Inorganic matter is naturally occurring but does not come from a living organism.

PROPERTIES OF SEDIMENTARY ROCKS

Five main properties help geologists determine what material a rock is made from and how it was formed. Geologists are scientists who study rocks.

Color: Sedimentary rocks come in many different colors, including grey, brown, black, red, green, and orange.

Texture: The size, shape, and arrangement of the

Quartz minerals have distinctive crystalline structures due to their chemical makeup.

particles that make up a rock.

Mineralogy: The inorganic mineral content contained within a rock, such as quartz or shiny mica.

Fossils: The remains of ancient plants or animals preserved in rock. Most fossils are found in sedimentary rock.

Structure: The large-scale arrangement of a rock formation.

Think About It

Geologists study the physical features and history of Earth. How would studying rocks answer questions about how Earth came to have its present shape and form?

STRATA

Sedimentary rock is formed in layers, which are called strata. (One single layer of rock is known as a stratum.) Strata pile on top of one another to form a structure called bedding, which makes up the shape of the rock formation. The shape of this bedding affects what humans can build on the rock, such as houses and roads.

Geologists learn about the history of Earth by studying the layers of rock in Earth's surface. The deepest strata are the oldest, and newer ones lie on

Strata of sedimentary rock are easily visible in this cliff side. Each layer can tell us something new.

Scientists take great care to avoid damaging rock formations and fossils while unearthing them.

←

top of them closer to the top. Each layer contains unique types of rock and fossils, showing what sorts of life-forms lived in different periods of Earth's past.

Compare and Contrast

Paleontologists are geologists who study fossils, the traces of prehistoric plants and animals embedded in sedimentary rock. How are they different from other geologists?

GEOLOGIC TIME

Most geologists agree that Earth started forming about 4.6 billion years ago. After about 700 million years, it developed a solid crust. Geologists use the term "geologic time" to describe the vast number of years that have passed since then.

Think About It

Earth's crust, which is covered by a thin surface of sedimentary rock, formed about four billion years ago. The oldest known fossils found in sedimentary rock are more than three billion years old!

Earth's surface has changed much since ancient times. This artwork shows long-ago volcanic activity.

By studying the strata of sedimentary rock that form Earth's surface, scientists can learn about the many different animals and plants that lived on Earth over time. They can also learn about geologic disasters and events that have caused changes in the shape of Earth's surface.

Ancient meteor impacts made major changes to Earth's surface. Some of these remain visible to this day as gigantic craters.

FOSSILS

Most fossils are found in sedimentary rock because its formation does not require high heat or pressure that might destroy fossilized remains. Fossils are preserved when the hard parts of a creature's body—such as bones or a shell—become incorporated into sediment that eventually forms rock, preserving their shape within the rock. Other fossils are formed through imprints in soft sediment that hardened into rock,

Fossilized sea life and wave patterns have left fascinating textures in this rock.

Much of what we know about dinosaurs—such as their likely appearance—stems from the study of fossils.

such as a dinosaur footprint in mud.

Fossils allow paleontologists to determine when the fossilized creature lived on Earth by dating the strata of rock in which the fossil was found.

Think About It

How might scientists learn about the life of a prehistoric creature based on its fossil? Could a paleontologist make a guess about the size of a dinosaur based on its fossilized footprint?

SEDIMENTOLOGY

Scientists known as sedimentologists study the materials that form sedimentary rock (sand, gravel, and mud). Sedimentologists also examine the processes that cause these substances to form rock. Learning about the ways that sedimentary rock forms in the present day helps scientists understand how older strata of rock formed in ancient times.

In order to understand how rocks are created, sedimentologists measure rock formations and investigate the materials rocks

Studying sedimentary rock requires organization and careful measurement.

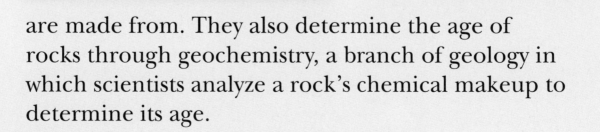

Sedimentology includes much lab work, including measuring and recording the properties of rock samples.

→

Think About It

How does studying the sediment that makes rock help scientists understand the processes that form rock? How could observing the movement of modern sand dunes teach sedimentologists about ancient sandstone formations?

are made from. They also determine the age of rocks through geochemistry, a branch of geology in which scientists analyze a rock's chemical makeup to determine its age.

SEDIMENTARY ENVIRONMENTS

The place in which a sedimentary rock forms is called its sedimentary environment, also known as a depositional environment.

The type of sediment, the surrounding conditions, and characteristics of the area determine these environments. Continental environments are ones where all depositions occur on land.

Transitional environments are where both marine and land processes are responsible for

An alluvial fan is a fan- or cone-shaped deposit of sediment. Sudden rainstorms or floods create alluvial fans in the desert.

Studying environments in which sedimentary rock forms helps sedimentologists understand how the characteristics of each environment contribute to the formation of rocks found there. Then, applying the same process in reverse, they may draw conclusions about long-ago environments in which ancient rock formations were created.

deposition, such as where a river feeds sediment into an ocean.

Marine environments include the seas and oceans. All of these sedimentary environments have their own subenvironments. Each can tell us different things about the distant past and how these current sediments were formed.

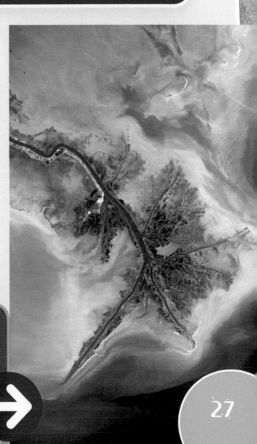

Environments that span both land and water are known as transitional environments.

SEDIMENTARY ROCK AND SOCIETY

Sedimentary rock's properties help sustain humanity and society in many ways. Sedimentary rock holds a large percentage of Earth's groundwater, which would otherwise soak up into soil. This rock type also generates deposits of coal and petroleum oils, which provide energy for human use. Copper, gold, silver, and precious gemstones are found within sedimentary

Coal is one sedimentary rock that provides a major energy source for human activities.

rock. Clay for use in ceramics and sculpture is found within sedimentary rock, and sedimentary stone is also used to create buildings and homes.

Studying sedimentary rock and rock strata is absolutely essential to the safe construction of roads, buildings, and other man-made structures. The formations of surface rock also assist scientists in predicting dangerous natural events like earthquakes.

Think About It

How would human life be different without the properties of—and products provided by—sedimentary rock?

Buildings cannot be built securely without a thorough understanding of the ground under them.

GLOSSARY

bedding The structural formation of sedimentary rock made up of layers of strata.

biochemical sedimentary rocks Sedimentary rocks formed from organic material.

chemical sedimentary rocks Sedimentary rocks formed from inorganic material.

clastic sedimentary rocks Sedimentary rocks formed from particles of sediment that are bonded together either by pressure or by minerals acting as cement.

conglomerates Sedimentary rocks made up of large fragments of sediment. These large fragments are held together by dissolved minerals that act as cement.

erosion The process by which fragments of rock are worn away by wind, water, and ice.

fossil A trace, a print, or the remains of a plant or animal of a past age preserved in rocks.

geochemistry The study of Earth's chemical composition, its rocks, and its minerals.

geologic time The billions of years since the planet Earth began developing.

geology The science that deals with Earth's history and its life, especially as recorded in rocks.

metamorphic rock Rock that was once one form of rock but changed to another due to the influence of heat or pressure.

rock cycle The endlessly repeating process in which old rock wears away or becomes transformed to create new types of rock.

FOR MORE INFORMATION

BOOKS

Blobaum, Cindy. *Geology Rocks!: 50 Hands-On Activities to Explore the Earth*
   (Kaleidoscope Kids). Charlotte, VT: Williamson Publishing, 1999.
Dee, Willa. *Unearthing Sedimentary Rocks* (Rocks: The Hard Facts). New York, NY:
   PowerKids Press, 2014.
Green, Dan. *Scholastic Discover More: Rocks and Minerals.* New York, NY: Scholastic
   Reference, 2013.
Hyde, Natalie. *What Are Sedimentary Rocks?* (Let's Rock!). New York, NY: Crabtree
   Publishing Company, 2010.
Tomecek, Steve. *National Geographic Kids Everything Rocks and Minerals: Dazzling
   Gems of Photos and Info That Will Rock Your World.* Washington, DC: National
   Geographic Children's Books, 2011.

WEBSITES

Because of the changing nature of Internet links, Rosen Publishing has developed an
online list of websites related to the subject of this book. This site is updated regularly.
Please use this link to access this list:

http://www.rosenlinks.com/GEOL/Sed

INDEX